Sorrento & the Amalfi Coast
Travel Guide

Quick Trips Series

No part of this publication may be reproduced, stored in a retrieval system, or transmitted, in any form or by any means without the prior written permission of the publisher, nor be otherwise circulated in any form of binding or cover other than that in which it is published and without similar condition being imposed on the subsequent purchaser. If there are any errors or omissions in copyright acknowledgements the publisher will be pleased to insert the appropriate acknowledgement in any subsequent printing of this publication. Although we have taken all reasonable care in researching this book we make no warranty about the accuracy or completeness of its content and disclaim all liability arising from its use.

Copyright © 2016, Astute Press
All Rights Reserved.

Table of Contents

SORRENTO & THE AMALFI COAST   5
- PLANNING YOUR STAY 12
- CLIMATE & WEATHER 15

SIGHTSEEING   17
- SORRENTO CATHEDRAL 17
- CORREALE DI TERANOVA ART MUSEUM 19
- POMPEII & HERCULANEUM 22
- MOUNT VESUVIUS 26
- CAPRI 31
- ISCHIA 33
- PROCIDA 35
- AMALFI 37
- PAESTUM 39
- PRAIANO 40
- SALERNO 42
- RAVELLO 43
- POSITANO 44
- PROTECTED MARINE RESERVE OF PUNTA CAMPANELLA 45

BUDGET TIPS   47
- ACCOMMODATION 47

Sorrento..48
  Ravello (Amalfi Coast)..................................49
  Pompeii..50
  Naples..50
 🌐 **PLACES TO EAT**..51
  Sant'anna da Emilia..................................51
  Zi' Antonio..52
  Taverna Azzura..53
  Gelateria Davide..53
 🌐 **SHOPPING**..54
  Macramé..54
  Limonoro..55
  De Cenzo..56

KNOW BEFORE YOU GO — 57

🌐 **ENTRY REQUIREMENTS** 57
🌐 **HEALTH INSURANCE** 57
🌐 **TRAVELLING WITH PETS** 58
🌐 **AIRPORTS** 58
🌐 **AIRLINES** 60
🌐 **CURRENCY** 61
🌐 **BANKING & ATMS** 61
🌐 **CREDIT CARDS** 61
🌐 **TOURIST TAXES** 62
🌐 **RECLAIMING VAT** 62
🌐 **TIPPING POLICY** 63
🌐 **MOBILE PHONES** 63
🌐 **DIALLING CODE** 64
🌐 **EMERGENCY NUMBERS** 64
🌐 **PUBLIC HOLIDAYS** 65

- Time Zone 66
- Daylight Savings Time 66
- School Holidays 66
- Trading Hours 67
- Driving Laws 67
- Drinking Laws 68
- Smoking Laws 69
- Electricity 69
- Tourist Information (TI) 70
- Food & Drink 70
- Websites 72

SORRENTO & THE AMALFI COAST TRAVEL GUIDE

Sorrento & the Amalfi Coast

Located in the southwestern region of Campania in southern Italy, Sorrento and the Amalfi Coastal towns are some of the most popular tourist destinations in Italy. Sorrento is 60km south of Naples and Amalfi is 12km further along the Amalfi Coast. The stunning seaside

SORRENTO & THE AMALFI COAST TRAVEL GUIDE

landscape with deep gorges and 'citrus-mountains' dotted with beautiful Italian architecture gives the region a picture postcard look.

The destination has been a favorite with tourists, from the common man to the famous, for over a hundred years. The Coast has featured in dozens of movies and has inspired many songs and operas for over a hundred years. Concerts held with the deep blue waters of the bay as the backdrop or food festivals with the famous citrus and wine products of the region have made Sorrento and the Amalfi Coast a favorite for tourists off all ages.

Sorrento is a city with settlements for over 2500 years. Although its present name comes from the Roman Surrentum, the earliest ruins found in the area are linked to the Oscis who had Greek lineage. It is believed that the city was found by Liparus, the grandson of the legendary Ulysses. The Greek influence is highlighted by the fact that the most important temples in Surrentum – Athena and Sirens – were dedicated to the gods from the Greek mythology. Surrentum was strategically a very safe city with the sea and gorges on one side and the mountains on the other.

Sorrento was ruled by a number of empires over the centuries. After the decline of the Western Roman Empire, it was ruled by the Ostrogoths, and then the Eastern Roman Empire (Byzantine) in the 8th century. With the fading of the Byzantine authority, Sorrento became an autonomous duchy – ruled independently by a duke. In the 12th century it was conquered by the Normans and was made a part of the Kingdom of Naples. The city's destiny looked up in the 19th century after

SORRENTO & THE AMALFI COAST TRAVEL GUIDE

becoming a part of the Neapolitan Republic. Trade routes not only increased business, the area also came to be identified as a hot spot for vacations, thus increasing tourism. Sorrento became a part of the Kingdom of Italy in 1861.

The Amalfi Coast is a short distance from Sorrento and is located in the Province of Salerno. This UNESCO World Heritage Site since 1997 is known for its natural landscape as well as its history. There are a number of towns located on the Amalfi Coast, including Amalfi, Positano, and Ravello, each a tourist magnet in itself. The main town in the Amalfi Coast is Amalfi – a 6th century town that became a maritime power house because of its strategic location and strong commercial standing in the region. Political rivalry in the 12th century and a devastating tsunami in the 14th century reduced the

SORRENTO & THE AMALFI COAST TRAVEL GUIDE

importance of Amalfi forever. One can still visit the Museum at the coast to have a glimpse of the huge vaults and the piers that were used to build and repair the warships. Even though it was never to gain an important place in the maritime world after the 14th century, Amalfi etched its place in the world of ships with an important discovery – the mariner's compass – an instrument that was to become the most important lifeline of adventurous seafarers.

Sorrento and Amalfi are connected by a beautiful scenic road that was built by the Romans. Known as the Amalfi Drive or the Strada Statale 163, it is carved on the mountain side and runs along the coast providing a magnificent view of the Tyrrhenian Sea on one side and the mountain drop on the other. The total stretch of the road is about 80 km (Sorrento and Amalfi are about 34 km

SORRENTO & THE AMALFI COAST TRAVEL GUIDE

apart) connecting the town of Positano to Salerno at the southern base of the peninsula.

Sorrento and Amalfi Coast are part of a very popular tourist network in south Italy. With a picturesque landscape (dominated by the Bay and Mount Vesuvius), historic architecture (like the Sorrento Cathedral), unique food (like the limoncello made from lemon, alcohol, and sugar), and an ever welcoming weather, the region has been a favorite with tourists from all corners of the globe.

Plays, processions, or pizza – the Sorrentine Peninsula has something or the other to engross and amaze the visitors.

There are 2 major processions in Sorrento, both on Good Friday. The first - the Procession of Our Lady of Sorrows

SORRENTO & THE AMALFI COAST TRAVEL GUIDE

by the Venerable Arciconfraternita of Saint Monica – starts the night before, Thursday (Holy Thursday) at 3:30 am. The ritual includes participants in hooded white gowns carrying Madonna to the different parts of town and the churches in search of her son. The 2 hour procession is accompanied by a male choir and a band. The 2nd procession - Procession of the Crucified Christ by the Venerable Arciconfraternita of the Death – is held in the evening of Good Friday. Participants are dressed in black hooded gowns and the ritual includes Madonna mourning the death of her son.

The traditional events of Amalfi include the feast days of St Andrew, the Byzantine New Year, and the annual regatta. The St Andrew's feasts are held in June (25 – 27) and November (30) to honor the city's patron saint. The Byzantine New Year's Eve is celebrated on August 31st

SORRENTO & THE AMALFI COAST TRAVEL GUIDE

every year. This 1000 year old ritual brings to life the whole town with medieval plays, mock duels, water races, and a historic costume parade. The annual Historical Regatta is held on the first Sunday of June. It is a rowing competition between the 4 maritime republics – Amalfi, Venice, Genoa, and Pisa. The event goes round from one town to another so Amalfi gets to host it once every 4 years.

Apart from the religious and historical events, visitors can enjoy musical shows and theaters through a number of productions. Various events are organized throughout the year like the Aperti per Ferie – a string of theater shows, musical gigs, and dance exhibitions in Casarlano – a municipality in Sorrento. Another venue is the Piano de Sorrento which organizes concerts and theatrical performances. The Napoli Theatre Festival held every

SORRENTO & THE AMALFI COAST TRAVEL GUIDE

summer brings performers from all corners of the world. The Sant' Antonio Abate Festival is held every winter and is a musical event promoting local Italian artists. Open air concerts with the beautiful bay as the backdrop are a must for music lovers, not only for the quality of music, but for the sheer aesthetic value. Popular events include the classical performances at the Jaranto's Bay and the Ravello Music Festival.

The Sorrentine Peninsula is also a place of gastronomical delight. The Mediterranean climate of the region is perfect for the growth of grapes and various citrus fruits. The white and red wines of Campania have captured the wine lovers' attention in the last few years with improved processing. The lemons of the area command a special mention. Almost double the size of the usual lemons, it has influenced many dishes and drinks over the centuries.

SORRENTO & THE AMALFI COAST TRAVEL GUIDE

Most popular amongst those is the limoncello liqueur. In fact, so popular is the lemon, there is a Festival of Lemons every summer. Food lovers can also visit the 'Piano…sweet Piano Food Festival' that has non-professional cooks participating in a cake making contest. The Mostra Mercato Prodotti Tipici Food Festival in summer is a celebration of local wine and food along with musical concerts. The Termini Carnival in February is a colorful family festival with clowns, jugglers, and musical shows.

🌐 Planning Your Stay

For those who are flying in, there are 2 airports – The Naples International Airport (IATA: NAP) - http://www.portal.gesac.it, and the Salerno Costa d'Amalfi Airport (IATA: QSR) - http://www.aeroportosalerno.it/. Sorrento is 54 km from NAP and 75 km from QSR. The

SORRENTO & THE AMALFI COAST TRAVEL GUIDE

town of Amalfi is 75 km from NAP and 45 km from QSR. Flyers mostly use NAP as there are more services and connections.

From the Napoli airport one can use the bus, train, or taxi service to get to their destination. Details of the bus service from the NAP airport can be found at - http://www.anm.it/default.php?ids=15&. Details of the taxi service and the rates can be found at - http://www.comune.napoli.it.

Sorrento is connected by a private rail link – Circumvesuviana- http://www.eavcampania.it/web/ to Napoli. The rail link runs along the coast providing a beautiful view of the scenery.

SORRENTO & THE AMALFI COAST TRAVEL GUIDE

The Sita Bus Service - http://www.sitabus.it/ - has regular bus connections to Sorrento and the Amalfi Coast from the airports and a number of neighboring town and cities.

Being a coastal area, this tourist region is also well connected by boat. There are regular services by http://www.alilauro.it/ and http://www.snav.it/ connecting Sorrento and Naples. The 1 hr ride is faster than by road and costs about €12. Tourists visiting Amalfi often use the boat service from Naples. Ferry services are also available from the towns of Capri and Salerno.

Although the road is very scenic, it is best to avoid driving as there can be very heavy traffic, especially during summer time. Renting a scooter is an option else it is best to use public transport as driving and parking can be a problem.

SORRENTO & THE AMALFI COAST TRAVEL GUIDE

Once in the area, one can see a number of major attractions by foot. There are bus services, mostly operated by Sita that takes one to some of the neighboring tourist attractions. Cycling is an option but the mountain roads can make it very tiring. Another option is to use the local bus or (car) lifts from the harbor to the town center. Lifts cost €1 and is used by locals and tourists alike.

Take a look at the area maps here:

Sorrento - http://goo.gl/maps/R3rLK

Amalfi Coast - http://goo.gl/maps/XNpWe

🌐 Climate & Weather

Sorrento and the Amalfi Coast experience a Mediterranean climate. This brings about warm summers

SORRENTO & THE AMALFI COAST TRAVEL GUIDE

and mild winters with rain. The summer temperature reaches 30 degrees Celsius during the months of Jun – Sep. Lows are around 16 – 18 degrees Celsius. Winter temperatures during the months Dec – Feb reach a high of around 14 degrees Celsius and the lows are around 3 – 5 degrees Celsius. Rainfall is highest between Oct – Feb with Oct & Nov being the wettest months with an average rainfall of about 130 mm – 163 mm. With the warm and dry summers, Sorrento and the Amalfi Coast are best visited during the summer months.

SORRENTO & THE AMALFI COAST TRAVEL GUIDE

Sightseeing

🌐 Sorrento Cathedral

Via Santa Maria della Pietà 44

80067 Sorrento (Na)

Tel: 0039 081 878 22 48

http://www.cattedralesorrento.it

The Cattedrale dei Santi Filippo e Giacomo or Sorrento Cathedral is a Catholic Church of the 11th century that was rebuilt in a Baroque style in the 15th century. Easily recognized for its 3-storey high bell tower with a clock, the cathedral has a very simple look on the outside. Once inside, it will amaze the visitor with beautifully crafted interior, high arches, and majestically painted ceiling by painter Giacomo Del Po.

SORRENTO & THE AMALFI COAST TRAVEL GUIDE

The original Sorrento Cathedral was built further upstream around 1st century AD. In the 10th century it was decided to bring the Cathedral within the city walls to its present location. The Cathedral was consecrated by Cardinal Riccardo de Albano and dedicated to Mother Mary in 1113. The Cathedral was destroyed in an attack by the Turks in 1558 and had to be completely rebuilt. It was transformed into a Baroque style church complete with pink marble columns and pedestals influenced from ancient pagan temples. Unfortunately, only the entry to the façade has survived the passage of time.

Inside, there are 3 naves with fourteen pillars. At the very end of the nave there is a Latin wooden crucifix. One can also see a 16th century marble altar, marble pulpit, and a Bishop's throne. The Cathedral has an 18th century organ by Nicola Mancino with intricate gilded carvings. The

Cathedral has fifteen chapels, some with beautiful Biblical paintings. The fourth chapel is dedicated to the first four bishops with their relics visible beneath the marble altar.

The Cathedral is open every day from 8:00 am – 12:30 pm and from 4:30 pm – 8:30 pm. Tourists are not allowed to enter when Mass is held; but one can enter the Chapter House Museum which is adjacent to the left wall of the Cathedral.

🌐 Correale di Teranova Art Museum

Via Correale

50 Sorrento (Na)

Tel: 0039 081 878 18 46

http://www.museocorreale.it/

SORRENTO & THE AMALFI COAST TRAVEL GUIDE

Located in the Sorrento town center, the Correale di Teranova Art Museum spreads over 24 rooms in a 4-storey Italian villa. The Museum, with its exquisite collection of art and artifacts captures the life and atmosphere of the Sorrentine past.

The Museum, opened in 1924, was the brainchild of 2 brothers Alfredo and Pompeo Correale, the last descendants of an aristocratic family of Sorrento. They directed through their will that their art collections be displayed in the Villa Correale in a Museum with their names.

The ground floor of the Museum is dedicated to the Correale family and to archeological findings related to the history of Sorrento. Exhibits include marbles and pottery from the Roman and Greek period. The first floor has a wide collection of paintings and furniture. Many of the paintings are by painters influenced by the Mannerism and Neapolitan style of art. The precious furnishings displayed include English and French styled cabinets that were used by the nobles of the period. The floor also has a stunning collection of mirrors with intricate gilded artwork.

The first 4 rooms of the second floor are dedicated to paintings of still life by Neapolitan artists. A part of the central hall has paintings showing the evolution of landscape paintings over the centuries. The rest of the floor is dedicated to a stunning collection of watches, glasses, and rare items. The fourth floor reflects the fine taste of the Correale brothers through the beautiful collection of porcelain, collected from all over Europe. The collection reflects the history and culture of fine arts of

SORRENTO & THE AMALFI COAST TRAVEL GUIDE

Europe from the middle ages to the industrial era. The Museum also has a library.

The Museum Villa, a work of art in itself, was the private residence of the Correale brothers. It is set amidst a beautiful garden of trees, some of which are centuries old. The garden leads to the Belvedere Terrace where one can have a beautiful view of the sea and the scenery of the Gulf of Naples.

The Museum is open 9:30 am – 6:30 pm from Tues – Sat. It closes at 1:30 pm on Sundays, public holidays, and during the winter months (Nov – Mar). It is closed on Mondays.

Ticket prices are: Adult – €8. Group discounts are available.

🌍 Pompeii & Herculaneum

A 25 minute train ride from Sorrento in the Circumvesuviana suburban railway transports one back in history by 2500 years to two cities that are famous not for their existence but for their destruction – Pompeii and Herculaneum. These Roman towns with thousand of inhabitants were laid to sleep forever in 79AD by a destructive volcanic eruption of the neighboring Mt Vesuvius.

Today, the two towns stand as memorials, not only of the life during that period but also as a proof of the wrath of nature. Each year, the towns draw millions of tourists and history buffs from all corners of the globe, taking them through a walk of Roman life and architecture. The City of Pompeii has been declared a UNESCO World Heritage

SORRENTO & THE AMALFI COAST TRAVEL GUIDE

Site and a World Monuments Watch (involved with the restoration of world monuments).

Pompeii was a rich resort city of the wealthy Romans and had many beautiful villas and groves along the slopes of Mt Vesuvius. Herculaneum, a neighboring town, was wealthier than Pompeii and had houses and villas made with finer and stronger material (one of the reasons that more intact houses were excavated in Herculaneum). Both the towns were established around 6th century BC. Pompeii, in fact, was quite modern for its age. The town was laid out in a grid lay-out planning and had an elaborate water system. The 3-stream water system flowed through lead pipes and connected with the public fountains, homes of the wealthy, and the public baths. The city was prone to minor earthquakes and flooding throughout its existence and inhabitants were used to the minor wraths of nature.

It was life as usual for the nearly 16000 inhabitants of the towns on August 24, 79AD. It was just a day after the Festival dedicated to the Roman God of Fire, including that of volcanoes! The first eruptions of the Vesuvius were around 1:00 pm. No living person in any of the towns had seen the Vesuvius erupt as it had not done so in the past few hundred years. There was enough time for all the inhabitants to escape, but having seen minor natural disasters, no one could predict the looming danger. When the lava started flowing, there was hardly any time for escape as it approached at a staggering speed of nearly 30m per second. In fact, studies have showed that the temperatures had risen to nearly 250 degrees Celsius from the eruption, enough to kill the humans and animals even in the shelter of their homes. Herculaneum suffered a different fate – the inhabitants were first killed by the toxic gases from the eruption and then buried by the lava. Pompeii was buried under nearly 2 – 4m of lava and rocks and Herculaneum under 23m of lava.

The 30 km high eruption was recorded in 2 letters by Pliny the Younger, a poet who witnessed the eruption. In memory of his accounts, volcanologists have named the first eruptions of any major volcano as 'plinian'. Excavations have unearthed not only houses, villas, household items, and public baths, but also relics of humans and animals of the region. Plaster casts were made to partially restore the shape and form of the bodies during their last moments. The towns today, stand as living museums and a snapshot of that fateful August 24th afternoon.

SORRENTO & THE AMALFI COAST TRAVEL GUIDE

Excavations have unearthed almost the complete towns and one can see a number of things in almost the exact form. Cobbled streets, the amphitheater, residential houses, taverns and mills, and a wine shop complete with the wine jars. The Villa of Venus, a wealthy residence with its beautiful frescoes and pillared façade deserves special mention.

If travelling from Sorrento, it would be a good idea to spend a day in Pompeii and then visit Herculaneum the following day which is about a 17 minute ride from Pompeii. There are 5 sites each costing €11, but a combined ticket to all 5 sites valid for 3 consecutive days cost €20.

SORRENTO & THE AMALFI COAST TRAVEL GUIDE

One can opt for the Campania ArteCard -

http://www.campaniartecard.it/ - for a discount.

Mount Vesuvius

Naples

Tel: 0039 081 865 39 11

http://www.epnv.it/pnv/home/index.asp

The most commanding view in the Gulf of Naples is that of a volcanic mountain that has been a tourist attraction for hundreds of years – Mt Vesuvius. Standing next to the shore, Mt Vesuvius is the smallest active volcano in the world. With nearly 300000 inhabitants living in the area, the Campanian region is regarded as the most densely populated volcanic region in the world. Looking from the sea towards the shore, Mt Vesuvius commands a panoramic view of the skyline, its peak often covered with clouds and vapor.

The highest point of the mountain – Mount Somma – reaches 1282 m above sea level with the current crater having a diameter of 650m and a depth of 230m. The large cone that makes up the Vesuvius is known as the Cono Grande. The slopes of the Vesuvius have remnants of the lava trails having experienced 3 minor eruptions in the 20th century itself.

Mt Vesuvius is inside the Vesuvius National Park (stretching 8842 hectares) and one can reach the top of the Vesuvius through 9 different trails in the Park. Trail No. 5 (Gran Cono) and Trail No. 6 (Strada Matrone) are regarded the best for a hike. While Gran Cono is a circular trail offering breathtaking views of the crater, the

SORRENTO & THE AMALFI COAST TRAVEL GUIDE

Strada Matrone offers a great view of the neighboring areas.

There are 13 municipalities within the Park boundary. Boscotrecase is close to Pompeii and is the starting point of Strada Matrone. It has a 17th century church, one of the oldest religious buildings in the Vesuvius area. Ercolano is the starting point of Via Vesuvio that crosses the path of the lava flow from the 1944 eruption. Although the town has some historic 18th century residences, it is best known for the volcanic ruins. The Massa di Somma, at the foot of the volcano has predominantly modern architecture as the original town was completely razed in the 1944 eruption.

The farming town of Ottavlano has been a favorite holiday destination for centuries with the landscape dotted with a number of 18th century churches. Pollena Trocchia is a very picturesque region with some surviving medieval period districts. Sant' Ananstasia is not only known for its copper craftsmanship, the parish church in the town is a revered Christian pilgrimage. San Gluseppe Vesuviano is the phoenix amongst the municipalities having been destroyed and rebuilt time and again amidst the fury of the volcanic eruptions.

The farming town Boscoreale is famous for its fruits and wines, a specialty of that region. San Sebastiano al Vesuvio, like the Massa di Somma, was also completely destroyed in the 1944 eruption except the 18th century St Sebastian Church, which survived miraculously, stands to date with its dominating white dome. Somma Vesuviana with its historical castle ruins and medieval roads is a must visit for history buffs.

SORRENTO & THE AMALFI COAST TRAVEL GUIDE

The 18th century town of Terzigno was named after the third stream of the lava and literally means – third fire. The town has grown in popularity for its wine production. Torre del Greco is not only famous for its coral production; it is also a site with immense historical importance with its centuries old churches and buildings. The town also offers some breathtaking views of the surroundings. The town of Trecase at the foot of the Vesuvius has some beautiful forest reserves that include cluster pine and ilex forests.

Due to the unique quality of the soil coupled with a favorable Mediterranean climate, the flora and fauna around the Vesuvius has developed vegetation with 610 varying species including 18 endemic ones. The mixed woodlands have a variety of oak, maple, chestnut, and alder trees. The mesophyll woodland has 20 species of orchids. One can also find 140 species of birds and 44 different species of butterflies. There are a number of treks and guided tours that nature lovers can choose from.

Mt Vesuvius is about 9 km from Naples and can be reached from Naples or Sorrento through the Circumvesuviana railway line. After getting down at Ercolano (Scavi), one can take the Vesuvius Express or the direct bus service that is offered by a number of companies. A one-way trip costs €10. One can also buy the €10 ticket for the crater entry from these transport service companies. One can also drive up the mountain by taking the Ercolano exit off the A3 Napoli-Salerno highway.

The region around Mt Vesuvius is not only one of picture-postcard beauty; it is also unique and famous for its gastronomic value. The mozzarella (made from buffalo milk), tomatoes, and seafood are highly recommended. The region is also famous for its wines, both red and white. Dotted with pubs and cafes, it is the perfect place to sip on some Campanian wine with the Vesuvius sunset.

Capri

http://www.capri.com/en

Your best friend may advice you not to go to Capri, because you may not want to come back! Located in south of the Gulf of Naples, 5 km from the coast, this small Italian island with a land area of only 10.4 sq km has been one of the world's most favorite islands for vacationing. The island was the honeymoon destination for the Greek shipping magnate Aristotle Onassis after his marriage with Jacqueline Kennedy. It has also been a favorite with many celebrities from Alexandre Dumas, Graham Greene, and Somerset Maugham to Sophia Loren, Julia Roberts, and Harrison Ford. In the summer time the island is chock-a-block with tourists and wedding parties, so one should be well prepared to wade through the crowded streets.

Capri can be reached directly by ferries and hydrofoils from Naples and Sorrento - http://www.capri.com/en/getting-here. Choose the left side of the ferry while sailing from Capri as one can get a beautiful view of the coastline. Of course, a more grand and expensive option is taking the helicopter. Once in town one can walk or use the public transport. Due to the

SORRENTO & THE AMALFI COAST TRAVEL GUIDE

high number of visitors, vehicles of non-residents are not allowed on the island in the summer months.

The hub of the Capri town center is distinct with its Italian terraces and pergolas. The Umberto I Square – nicknamed piazetta – is dominated by the Santo Stefano Baroque Church. To the right of the Church is the 14th century Palazzo Cerio. Architecture enthusiasts would enjoy the 14th century Caprese architecture of the Certosa di San Giacomo complex.

The neighboring Gardens of Augustus leads to the Marina Piccola through the via Krupp. The walk to the belvedere of Tragara overlooking the Marina is regarded as the most popular walk in the island with breathtaking views. The other inhabited part of the island, Anacapri has the historic Roman Villa Jovis commissioned by Emperor

Tiberius, one of the first patrons of the island. Other villas in the area are Villa Astarita, Damecuta, and Villa San Michele, each with its own trademark beauty.

Holidaying in Capri is not complete without a visit to the Blue Grotto – a stalactite cave with a stunning geological phenomenon. The light is reflected in such a manner in the crystalline waters of the 54m long cave that it emits a blur hue with silver reflections. The experience is stunning and, as Alexandre Dumas wrote – too marvelous to describe.

Ischia

http://www.ischia.it/en

Ischia is the largest island in the Gulf of Naples and is a

SORRENTO & THE AMALFI COAST TRAVEL GUIDE

popular tourist destination all year round primarily for its welcoming climate.

Many consider Ischia to be more beautiful than the popular island of Capri. The 46.3 sq km island attracts nearly 6 million tourists every year. The island, located in the northern end of the Gulf of Naples, is famous for its thermal spas, volcanic mud, beaches, and food.

Ischia is the most popular hub for thermal baths in the volcanic region. With 29 basins and myriads of mineral springs, and with the breathtaking backdrop of the beaches and the mountains, the thermal baths have made the island a tourist magnet. The main town of the island of Ischia is (also) called Ischia. It has 2 main hubs – the Port with its popular thermal baths, and the fortified

SORRENTO & THE AMALFI COAST TRAVEL GUIDE

Ponte with the dominating Aragonese Castle – the most visited tourist attraction on the island.

The island also has a number of gardens namely the La Mortella Gardens, Ravino Gardens, Corbaro Park, and the Eden Garden. The island has over half a dozen museums including the Santa Restituta Museum, the La Colombaia Museum, and the Villa Arbusto Museum. One can also trek up the 788m high Mt Epomeo and enjoy Ischia's claim to fame – the stunningly breathtaking scenery. The island has also featured in a number of movies including The Talented Mr. Ripley and the classic Cleopatra.

 Procida

http://www.procida.net/

SORRENTO & THE AMALFI COAST TRAVEL GUIDE

Procida is the smallest of the Phlegraean Archipelago having a land area of only 4.1 sq km.

Inhabited by about 10000 people, the island off the coast of Naples lies close to the island of Ischia. Procida has direct ferry connections with Naples, Ischia, and Pozzuoli through a number of companies - http://www.procida.it/orari.htm.

This tiny island with a jagged coast has a satellite island – Vivara – linked with a bridge. Procida is not as touristy as many of its neighboring islands and is a perfect getaway for those who are looking for a quiet holiday in the Bay of Naples. The island has a rich architectural history mostly with a Greek origin. The Vivara islet is known for its archeological excavations. Vivara is protected by the

SORRENTO & THE AMALFI COAST TRAVEL GUIDE

WWF and one needs permission from the City of Procida to visit it.

The Port of Sancio Cattalico, popularly known as the Marina Grande is the entry port for the island. The port area is dotted with brightly colored sea-facing houses as if a rainbow of colors is flowing through those. This fishing village is dominated by a castle and the Terra Murata, the highest point in the island. The medieval village with its gardens and architecture has remained almost unchanged for nearly 3 centuries. Beach lovers can head to the Marina di Chiaiolella or the Procida lido for a swim. The island has a total of 6 beaches.

Being a fishing town, one should not miss the fresh fish that is a part of the Procida cuisine. One can also try the traditional stewed rabbit and the spaghetti with sea-urchins.

Amalfi

http://www.amalfitouristoffice.it

The town of Amalfi located in the Campania region of south Italy is a popular destination on the Amalfi Coast and is a UNESCO World Heritage Site. Cradled inside a deep ravine between Mount Auereo and Mount Tabor, the town is surrounded by magnificent cliffs which open up to the Bay of Naples. The pastel colored houses add a mystic charm to the town that was once the capital of the maritime republic.

Amalfi is connected by road with neighboring towns like Sorrento (through the famous Amalfi Drive), Praiano,

SORRENTO & THE AMALFI COAST TRAVEL GUIDE

Ravello, and Napoli. Although the distance from the neighboring cities is not much, the summertime traffic can make the journey very slow and frustrating. Amalfi can be reached by ferry from Naples, Positano, and Sorrento. Ferries are operated by the Metro del Mare and the Coop Sant'Andrea. The Circumvesuviana train service connects Amalfi with other towns in the Amalfi Coast.

Amalfi has a number of tourist attractions. One of the most popular is the Amalfi Cathedral or the Cathedral of St. Andrew. Construction of the Cathedral started in the 9th century and was completed in the 19th century. The Romanesque Baroque monument has an Arab-influenced exterior with a basilica and cloister having medieval murals. A crypt contains the relics of St Andrew the Apostle. The impressive façade, bell tower, and the

SORRENTO & THE AMALFI COAST TRAVEL GUIDE

medieval bronze doors make the Cathedral stand out in the busy Piazza Duomo.

The Museum of the Compass and Maritime Duchy of Amalfi - http://www.museoarsenaleamalfi.it/4/ - was opened in December 2010 and exhibits relics and maritime models that once made Amalfi, the first maritime republic, a major town in south Italy. The Emerald Grotto cave near the coast transports the visitor to a magical trance with its natural display of colors brought about by the reflection of natural light on the crystalline waters and stalactite surfaces. There is a €5 entry fee for the cave.

Amalfi is also popular for guided tours and excursions and one can choose from many including the 'That's Amore Cycling Excursion' and the Charter La Dolce Vita.

Amalfi is also a region of gastronomic delight and visitors should try the traditional sawfish, the parmigiane, pepper laganelle, and the shrimp fusilli.

Paestum

Located 85 km south east of Naples in the Campania region of south Italy, the Greek town of Paestum is frequented by tourists for its centuries old ruins from the Greek civilization. The partially excavated town is close to the Tyrrhenian coast. Excavated findings include 3 well preserved Greek temples, a city wall with tower ruins, and many statues and household items. A museum in the site displays the many smaller items that were found in the site.

One can get to Paestum by train from Salerno or Naples; Paestum has its own railway station. Ferry services are available in the summer months from Salerno, Naples, Positano, and Amalfi. There a number of private coach services that run from various parts of town and charge around €9 for a round trip.

There are a number of restaurants in the area and one can also visit the beach which is a 30-minute walk. The curios shops of the area are some of the cheapest in the Amalfi Coast.

Praiano

Located in the Amalfi Coast between the towns of Amalfi and Positano, is the quiet and beautiful fishing town of Praiano. Praiano, which means 'open sea' in Latin, is an apt name for this town as one can have panoramic views of the Bay from different viewpoints in the town.

SORRENTO & THE AMALFI COAST TRAVEL GUIDE

Praiano was a fashionable resort town during the maritime heydays of the Amalfi Coast. Today, in Praiano, one can have the feel of a medieval village and yet enjoy the facilities of the modern day. The crystal clear water of the Marina di Praia – its main beach – is surrounded by eroded cliffs. The medieval Torre a Mare watchtower overlooking the blue waters brings a rustic charm to the coastline.

The Church and convent of Santa Maria a Castro is set on a hillside 365 m above sea level that provided the peace and calm sought by the monks for their prayers. The 18th century Baroque styled St Luke Cathedral is decorated with the traditional maiolica tiles – a popular work of art of the Amalfi Coast region. Praiano, in fact, is a good spot to buy maiolica tile curios at a cheaper price than the neighboring Amalfi Coastal towns.

One can get to Praiano using the Sita bus service which has frequent connections running from the neighboring towns. Scooters are available for rent and are a pleasant ride through the scenic winding roads. Once in the city, one can see the attractions by foot.

Salerno

http://www.turismoinsalerno.it/salerno_e.htm

Located in the Gulf of Salerno, Salerno is a city and commune in the Campania region of south Italy. The city rose into political prominence when it was the administrative capital of Italy between February and August 1944 during World War II.

SORRENTO & THE AMALFI COAST TRAVEL GUIDE

The city was a great centre of learning in the 16th century. Today, it is an important cultural centre and has a growing popularity as a tourist destination. The city is divided into the medieval sector, the planned 19th century district, and the densely populated post war residential area.

Attractions in the city include the Salerno Cathedral - http://www.cattedraledisalerno.it/. Built in the 12th century the Cathedral also has a museum that houses beautiful artwork from different ages. Another popular attraction is the Castello Arechi, a 7th century castle that provides magnificent panoramic views of the city and the sea.

Salerno can be reached directly by bus, train, and ferries from neighboring towns as well as Naples.

Ravello

http://www.comune.ravello.sa.it/

Located in the hills above Amalfi, the town and commune of Ravello gives a bird's eye view of the stunning landscape of the Amalfi Coast and the Bay of Salerno. Perched atop the mountains, the town has been a favorite to many celebrities from across the globe.

Popular attractions in the town include the Villa Cimbrone - http://www.villacimbrone.com/. The Villa, now a refurbished hotel has attracted the famous and the powerful over the years including Winston Churchill, D H Lawrence, and Virginia Woolf. The exquisitely maintained public garden (€6) is open from 9:00 am till sunset.

The gateway and the passage are adorned with beautiful statues and plaques. The Villa Rufolo - http://villarufolo.it/ - is a palatial private estate with a beautiful garden overlooking the Bay. It was during a visit to the Villa that German composer Robert Wagner was inspired to compose the Parsifal. This prompted the open-air concert – the annual Ravello Music Festival - that is held in honor of Wagner. The town is also known for handcrafted items and is a good place to buy small works of art.

One can get to Ravello through the Sita bus connections. Most of the bus and ferry connections are to Amalfi which is the closest major town. The town is small enough to be explored by foot.

Positano

http://www.positanonline.it

An important port of the Amalfi Republic in the medieval times, Positano today, is a village and commune with stunning views of the coastline that has made it a major tourist stop in the Amalfi Coast.

The beauty of Positano has been featured in a number of movies including the popular Hollywood hits Under the Tuscan Sun and Only You. Perched on the slope of a hill, Positano looks like a mountain with a blanket of multi-colored houses.

Tourist attractions, other than the village as a whole, include the Santa Maria Assunta Church housing the 13th century Byzantine icon – Madonna di Positano. Positano is also a great place to shop – colorful silk items and traditional painted tiles are popular with the tourists.

🌐 Protected Marine Reserve of Punta Campanella

http://www.puntacampanella.org/

Stretching 30 km from the Gulf of Naples to the Gulf of Salerno, the Reserve includes a number of islets, reefs, and grottoes that attract tourists for their beauty. The beauty of the Reserve is not only what is visible above water, but also the underwater world with its myriad varieties of multi-colored flora and fauna, making it a popular area for snorkeling and scuba diving. The islets with the typical Mediterranean vegetation are also home to a number of endemic species – both flora and fauna. Jeranto Bay deserves special mention with its deep grottoes and sightings of rare birds including the buzzard and the peregrine falcon.

SORRENTO & THE AMALFI COAST TRAVEL GUIDE

Budget Tips

🌐 Accommodation

There are quite a few places to stay in the region around Sorrento. Your best bet is to do your research before your visit, and decide how many days you'd like to spend in each location. Here are a few places to get you started.

SORRENTO & THE AMALFI COAST TRAVEL GUIDE

Sorrento

L'Angolo di Paradiso: One option to consider when you stay in Sorrento is to try a hotel in the Agriturismo movement. This movement aims to place visitors in local homes and farms, for a unique and ecologically sound housing option. L'Angolo di Paradiso, located right smack in the middle of Sorrento, is a beautiful farm surrounded by olives, lemons, and oranges. You can open your window and just feel the mixture of the salt water and lemon trees splash up against your face. There are six bedrooms here, as well as a restaurant that serves local and the freshest of fresh food you could possibly imagine. Breakfast is included, as well, so you can stock up for your busy day of touring.

Address: Via Monticelli, 2 c/o Il Corso Italia 333 - Sorrento

80067

http://www.agriturismo.it/en/farmhouse/campania/naples/LAngolodiParadiso-6190811/contact.html

Another good option, but if you want a "standard" hotel room, with no farm in sight, is the Hotel Il Nido, which has decent prices and has a beautiful view of the sea.

Address: Via Nastro Verde, 62

80067 Sorrento, Province of Naples, Italy

Telephone: 081 8782766

http://www.ilnido.it/

Ravello (Amalfi Coast)

Bed and Breakfast I Limoni: This Bed and Breakfast is in Ravello, which is a good place to stay on your tour of the Amalfi Coast. This is up a hill some ways, but is a great budget choice, and is actually part of a farm that produces lemons. Want to bet they make some great limoncello there? Also included is breakfast.

Address: Via Gradoni 14, San Cosma, Ravello

Telephone: 089 858056

www.bb-ilimoni.com

Pompeii

Hotel Apollo Pompeii is a nice, budget hotel located very close to the ruins of the city, so at the end of a long day of dusty walking, you can kick back and relax in your room, or in one of the hotels restaurants.

Address: Via Carlo Alberto 18, Pompeii

Telephone: 081 863 0309

http://www.hotelapollopompei.com/

Naples

Bed and Breakfast Bonapace Porta Nolana: This is close to the central station of Naples, so you can arrive then directly afterwards kick off your shoes and unpack. This is a clean, cheap option for those of you wanting to stay in the center of city, which has easy access to the port for trips to Capri, or up the hill to the shopping and restaurants in the Vomero District.

Address: Via San Cosmo Fuori Porta Nolana 4 - Naples

Telephone: 877-662-6988

http://www.bonapaceaccomodation.com/

🌐 Places to Eat

It is difficult to choose just a few recommendations for where to eat in the Sorrento area. If you're lucky, your guide along the coast of Amalfi will lead you to a restaurant tucked away in the hills, or on a secluded beach somewhere. Here are some tried and true choices for your time in beautiful Sorrento.

Sant'anna da Emilia

Sant'anna da Emilia is a charming place to get a delicious local meal. It is modestly priced, and is actually located in a former boat shed, adding to its historical appeal. Don't expect any pricey or sophisticated meals here; this trattoria is focused on serving fresh, local foods such as spaghetti with mussels or gnocchi, Sorrento-style. Pair your meal with the house wine, red or white, and sit back and enjoy. Reservations are usually not possible, so arrive before you want to eat if you come in tourist season, or be prepared to wait.

Address: Via Marina Grande 62, Sorrento

Telephone: 081 807 2720

Zi'Antonio

Zi'Antonio, which translates to "Uncle Tony" is a great option for those of you wanting to eat in the fishing village of Sorrento. It is small, and quaint, and its tiny size allows for personalized service at modest process. What makes this restaurant special is its private taxi service, which will send a car to your hotel and drive you back again (just make sure to tip the driver). Expect well-cooked local dishes and a long, lazy meal.

Address: Via Luigi De Maio, 11 – 80067, Sorrento

Telephone: 081 8781623

http://www.zintonio.it/

SORRENTO & THE AMALFI COAST TRAVEL GUIDE

Taverna Azzura

For a lovely place to eat after bathing to your heart's content in Marina Grande, try Taverna Azzura. It's known for its fried squid, a local favorite, and is located right on the water's edge. It is an extremely short walk from Piazza Tasso, and you will find it small but popular, so arrive ready to wait, or sit on the beach with a bottle of beer and await the local delicacies that will be sampling at dinner. A good idea, if you like seafood, is to try the catch of the day, which will always be prepared very lightly; sautéed with butter and garlic, and perhaps some lemon.

Address: 166 Marina Grande, Sorrento

Telephone: 081 877 2510

Website: www.taverna_azzurra.it

Gelateria Davide

No trip to Italy is complete without at least one gelato (ice cream.) One of the best places to sample some gelato on your journey is the Gelateria Davide. He's been in business since 1957, and you'll find this an ideal place to relax after a long day's touring. Try a coffee while you're there, or a sandwich or cake if you're hungry for more than ice cream.

Address: Sorrento Via P.R. Giuliani, 41 - Sorrento

Telephone: 081 8781337

http://www.davideilgelato.com/

🌎 Shopping

Tourists have been coming to shop on the Amalfi coast for centuries. From pottery to jewelry, to fabrics and fresh produce and fish, there is no shortage of things to open your purse strings for in Sorrento. So if you're a bit sunburnt and tired of the beach, head back into town and check out the following places:

Macramé

Macramé is located a few steps away from the historic Piazza Tazzo, and is a perfect place to look for lady's fashion, including hats, coats, bags, scarves, and gloves. This store has been open for quite some time, so it is fun to think of what famous people have shopped here before you.

Address: Via Luigi De Maio, 28 80067 Sorrento

Telephone: 081 8773114

http://www.sorrentotour.it/macrame/

Limonoro

It would be a sin to come all the way to Sorrento and at least not sample the local liquor, Limoncello. It probably would be just as bad not to come home with some for your friends and family. Head to Limonoro to find all sorts of lemon liquors and sweets, and other local delicacies to either bring back for your loved ones or keep just for yourself.

Address: Via San Cesareo, 49/53 0067 Sorrento

Telephone: 081 8785348

www.limonoro.it

De Cenzo

If you want to go home with some of Sorrento's beautiful ceramics, then look no further than De Cenzo, which specializes in handicrafts such as ceramics and paintings.

SORRENTO & THE AMALFI COAST TRAVEL GUIDE

Even if you don't go home with anything, it is a special treat to walk through the aisles of this store, gazing at crafts that are just as gorgeous as the treasures you could find in a museum.

Address: Via Tasso, 23 80067 Sorrento

Telephone: 081 8784757

www.decenzo.it

Know Before You Go

🌐 Entry Requirements

By virtue of the Schengen agreement, travellers from other countries in the European Union do not need a visa when visiting Italy. Additionally Swiss travellers are also exempt. Visitors from certain other countries such as the USA, Canada, Japan, Israel, Australia and New Zealand do not need visas if their stay in Italy does not exceed 90 days. When entering Italy you will be required to make a declaration of presence, either at the airport, or at a police station within eight days of arrival. This applies to visitors from other Schengen countries, as well as those visiting from non-Schengen countries.

🌐 Health Insurance

Citizens of other EU countries are covered for emergency health care in Italy. UK residents, as well as visitors from Switzerland are covered by the European Health Insurance Card (EHIC), which can be applied for free of charge. Visitors from non-Schengen countries will need to show proof of private health insurance that is valid for the duration of their stay in

Italy (that offers at least €37,500 coverage), as part of their visa application. No special vaccinations are required.

🌐 Travelling with Pets

Italy participates in the Pet Travel Scheme (PETS) which allows UK residents to travel with their pets without requiring quarantine upon re-entry. Certain conditions will need to be met. The animal will have to be microchipped and up to date on rabies vaccinations. In the case of dogs, a vaccination against canine distemper is also required by the Italian authorities. When travelling from the USA, your pet will need to be microchipped or marked with an identifying tattoo and up to date on rabies vaccinations. An EU Annex IV Veterinary Certificate for Italy will need to be issued by an accredited veterinarian. On arrival in Italy, you can apply for an EU pet passport to ease your travel in other EU countries.

🌐 Airports

Fiumicino – Leonardo da Vinci International Airport (FCO) is one of the busiest airports in Europe and the main international airport of Italy. It is located about 35km southwest of the historical quarter of Rome. Terminal 5 is used for trans-Atlantic and international flights, while Terminals 1, 2 and 3 serve mainly for domestic flights and medium haul flights to

SORRENTO & THE AMALFI COAST TRAVEL GUIDE

other European destinations. Before Leonardo da Vinci replaced it, the **Ciampino–G. B. Pastine International Airport** (CIA) was the main international airport servicing Rome and Italy. It is one of the oldest airports in the country still in use. Although it declined in importance, budget airlines such as Ryanair boosted its air traffic in recent years. The airport is used by Wizz Air, V Bird, Helvetic, Transavia Airlines, Sterling, Ryanair, Thomsonfly, EasyJet, Air Berlin, Hapag-Lloyd Express and Carpatair.

Milan Malpensa Airport (MXP) is the largest of the three airports serving the city of Milan. Located about 40km northwest of Milan's city center, it connects travellers to the regions of Lombardy, Piedmont and Liguria. **Milan Linate Airport** (LIN) is Milan's second international airport. **Venice Marco Polo Airport** (VCE) provides access to the charms of Venice. **Olbia Costa Smeralda Airport** (OLB) is located near Olbia, Sardinia. Main regional airports are **Guglielmo Marconi Airport** (BLQ), an international airport servicing the region of Bologna, **Capodichino Airport** at Naples (NAP), **Pisa International Airport** (PSA), formerly Galileo Galilei Airport, the main airport serving Tuscany, **Sandro Pertini Airport** near Turin (TRN), **Cristoforo Colombo** in Genoa (GOA), **Punta Raisi Airport** in Palermo (PMO), **Vincenzo Bellini Airport** in Catania (CTA) and **Palese Airport** in Bari (BRI).

SORRENTO & THE AMALFI COAST TRAVEL GUIDE

🌐 Airlines

Alitalia is the flag carrier and national airline of Italy. It has a subsidiary, Alitalia CityLiner, which operates short-haul regional flights. Air Dolomiti is a regional Italian based subsidiary of of the Lufthansa Group. Meridiana is a privately owned airline based at Olbia in Sardinia.

Fiumicino - Leonardo da Vinci International Airport serves as the main hub for Alitalia, which has secondary hubs at Milan Linate and Milan Malpensa Airport. Alitalia CityLiner uses Fiumicino – Leonardo da Vinci International Airport as main hub and has secondary hubs at Milan-Linate, Naples and Trieste. Fiumicino – Leonardo da Vinci International Airport is also one of two primary hubs used by the budget Spanish airline Vueling. Milan Malpensa Airport is one of the largest bases for the British budget airline EasyJet. Venice Airport serves as an Italian base for the Spanish budget airline, Volotea, which provides connections mainly to other destinations in Europe. Olbia Costa Smeralda Airport (OLB), located near Olbia, Sardinia is the primary base of Meridiana, a private Italian Airline in partnership with Air Italia and Fly Egypt.

🌐 Currency

Italy's currency is the Euro. It is issued in notes in denominations of €500, €200, €100, €50, €20, €10 and €5.

Coins are issued in denominations of €2, €1, 50c, 20c, 10c, 5c, 2c and 1c.

🌐 Banking & ATMs

Using ATMs or Bancomats, as they are known in Italy, to withdraw money is simple if your ATM card is compatible with the MasterCard/Cirrus or Visa/Plus networks. There is a €250 limit on daily withdrawals. Italian machines are configured for 4-digit PIN numbers, although some machines will be able to handle longer PIN numbers. Bear in mind some Bancomats can run out of cash over weekends and that the more remote villages may not have adequate banking facilities so plan ahead.

🌐 Credit Cards

Credit cards are valid tender in most Italian businesses. While Visa and MasterCard are accepted universally, most tourist oriented businesses also accept American Express and Diners Club. Credit cards issued in Europe are smart cards that that are fitted with a microchip and require a PIN for each transaction. This means that a few ticket machines, self-service vendors and other businesses may not be configured to accept the older magnetic strip credit cards. Do remember to advise your bank or credit card company of your travel plans before leaving.

SORRENTO & THE AMALFI COAST TRAVEL GUIDE

🌍 Tourist Taxes

Tourist tax varies from city to city, as each municipality sets its own rate. The money is collected by your accommodation and depends on the standard of accommodation. A five star establishment will levy a higher amount than a four star or three star establishment. You can expect to pay somewhere between €1 and €7 per night, with popular destinations like Rome, Venice, Milan and Florence charging a higher overall rate. In some regions, the rate is also adjusted seasonally. Children are usually exempt until at least the age of 10 and sometimes up to the age of 18. In certain areas, disabled persons and their companions also qualify for discounted rates. Tourist tax is payable directly to the hotel or guesthouse before the end of your stay.

🌍 Reclaiming VAT

If you are not from the European Union, you can claim back VAT (Value Added Tax) paid on your purchases in Italy. The VAT rate in Italy is 21 percent and this can be claimed back on your purchases if certain conditions are met. The merchant needs to be partnered with a VAT refund program. This will be indicated if the shop displays a "Tax Free" sign. The shop assistant will fill out a form for reclaiming VAT. When you submit this at the airport, you will receive your refund.

🌍 Tipping Policy

If your bill includes the phrase "coperto e servizio", that means that a service charge or tip is already included. Most waiting staff in Italy are salaried workers, but if the service is excellent, a few euros extra would be appreciated.

🌍 Mobile Phones

Most EU countries, including Italy use the GSM mobile service. This means that most UK phones and some US and Canadian phones and mobile devices will work in Italy. While you could check with your service provider about coverage before you leave, using your own service in roaming mode will involve additional costs. The alternative is to purchase an Italian SIM card to use during your stay in Italy.

Italy has four mobile networks. They are TIM, Wind, Vodafone and Tre (3) and they all provide pre-paid services. TIM offers two tourist options, both priced at €20 (+ €10 for the SIM card) with a choice of two packages - 2Gb data, plus 200 minutes call time or internet access only with a data allowance of 5Gb. Vodafone, Italy's second largest network offers a Vodafone Holiday package including SIM card for €30. They also offer the cheapest roaming rates. Wind offers an Italian Tourist pass for €20 which includes 100 minutes call time and 2Gb data and can be extended with a restart option for an extra €10.

SORRENTO & THE AMALFI COAST TRAVEL GUIDE

To purchase a local SIM card, you will need to show your passport or some other form of identification and provide your residential details in Italy. By law, SIM registration is required prior to activation. Most Italian SIM cards expire after a 90 day period of inactivity. When dialling internationally, remember to use the (+) sign and the code of the country you are connecting to.

🌐 Dialling Code

The international dialling code for Italy is +39.

🌐 Emergency Numbers

Police: 113
Fire: 115
Ambulance: 118
MasterCard: 800 789 525
Visa: 800 819 014

🌐 Public Holidays

1 January: New Year's Day (Capodanno)
6 January: Day of the Epiphany (Epifania)
March-April: Easter Monday (Lunedì dell'Angelo or Pasquetta)
25 April: Liberation Day (Festa della Liberazione)

1 May: International Worker's Day (Festa del Lavoro / Festa dei Lavoratori)

2 June: Republic Day (Festa della Repubblica)

15 August: Assumption Day (Ferragosto / Assunta)

1 November: All Saints Day (Tutti i santi / Ognissanti)

8 December: Immaculate Conception (Immacolata Concezione / Immacolata)

25 December: Christmas Day (Natale)

26 December: St Stephen's Day (Santo Stefano)

A number of Saints days are observed regionally throughout the year.

🌐 Time Zone

Italy falls in the Central European Time Zone. This can be calculated as Greenwich Mean Time/Coordinated Universal Time (GMT/UTC) +2; Eastern Standard Time (North America) -6; Pacific Standard Time (North America) -9.

🌐 Daylight Savings Time

Clocks are set forward one hour on 29 March and set back one hour on 25 October for Daylight Savings Time.

🌐 School Holidays

The academic year begins in mid September and ends in mid June. The summer holiday is from mid June to mid September, although the exact times may vary according to region. There are short breaks around Christmas and New Year and also during Easter. Some regions such as Venice and Trentino have an additional break during February for the carnival season.

🌐 Trading Hours

Trading hours for the majority of shops are from 9am to 12.30pm and then again from 3.30pm to 7.30pm, although in some areas, the second shift may be from 4pm to 8pm instead. The period between 1pm and 4pm is known in Italy as the *riposo*. Large department shops and malls tend to be open from 9am to 9pm, from Monday to Saturday. Post offices are open from 8.30am to 1.30pm from Monday to Saturday. Most shops and many restaurants are closed on Sundays. Banking hours are from 8.30am to 1.30pm and then again from 3pm to 4pm, Monday to Friday. Most restaurants are open from noon till 2.30pm and then again from 7pm till 11pm or midnight, depending on the establishment. Nightclubs open around 10pm, but only liven up after midnight. Closing times vary, but will generally be between 2am and 4am. Museum hours vary, although major sights tend to be open continuously and often up to 7.30pm. Many museums are closed on Mondays.

🌐 Driving Laws

The Italians drive on the right hand side of the road. A driver's licence from any of the European Union member countries is valid in Italy. Visitors from non-EU countries will require an International Driving Permit that must remain current throughout the duration of their stay in Italy.

The speed limit on Italy's autostrade is 130km per hour and 110km per hour on main extra-urban roads, but this is reduced by 20km to 110km and 90km respectively in rainy weather. On secondary extra-urban roads, the speed limit is 90km per hour; on urban highways, it is 70km per hour and on urban roads, the speed limit is 50km per hour. You are not allowed to drive in the ZTL or Limited Traffic Zone (or *zona traffico limitato* in Italian) unless you have a special permit.

Visitors to Italy are allowed to drive their own non-Italian vehicles in the country for a period of up to six months. After this, they will be required to obtain Italian registration with Italian licence plates. Italy has very strict laws against driving under the influence of alcohol. The blood alcohol limit is 0.05 and drivers caught above the limit face penalties such as fines of up to €6000, confiscation of their vehicles, suspension of their licenses and imprisonment of up to 6 months. Breathalyzer tests are routine at accident scenes.

🌍 Drinking Laws

The legal drinking age in Italy is 16. While drinking in public spaces is allowed, public drunkenness is not tolerated. Alcohol is sold in bars, wine shops, liquor stores and grocery shops.

🌍 Smoking Laws

In 2005, Italy implemented a policy banning smoking from public places such as bars, restaurants, nightclubs and working places, limiting it to specially designated smoking rooms. Further legislation banning smoking from parks, beaches and stadiums is being explored.

🌍 Electricity

Electricity: 220 volts

Frequency: 50 Hz

Italian electricity sockets are compatible with the Type L plugs, a plug that features three round pins or prongs, arranged in a straight line. An alternate is the two-pronged Type C Euro adaptor. If travelling from the USA, you will need a power converter or transformer to convert the voltage from 220 to 110, to avoid damage to your appliances. The latest models of many laptops, camcorders, mobile phones and digital cameras are dual-voltage with a built in converter.

🌐 Tourist Information (TI)

There are tourist information (TI) desks at each of the terminals of the Leonardo da Vinci International Airport, as well as interactive Information kiosks with the latest touch-screen technology. In Rome, the tourist office can be found at 5 Via Parigi, near the Termini Station and it is identified as APT, which stands for Azienda provinciale del Turismo. Free maps and brochures of current events are available from tourist kiosks.

Several of the more tourist-oriented regions of Italy offer tourist cards that include admission to most of the city's attractions. While these cards are not free, some offer great value for money. A variety of tourism apps are also available online.

🌐 Food & Drink

Pasta is a central element of many typically Italian dishes, but there are regional varieties and different types of pasta are matched to different sauces. Well known pasta dishes such as lasagne and bolognaise originated in Bologna. Stuffed pasta is popular in the northern part of Italy, while the abundance of

SORRENTO & THE AMALFI COAST TRAVEL GUIDE

seafood and olives influences southern Italian cuisine. As far as pizza goes, the Italians differentiate between the thicker Neapolitan pizza and the thin crust Roman pizza, as well as white pizza, also known as focaccia and tomato based pizza. Other standards include minestrone soup, risotto, polenta and a variety of cheeses, hams, sausages and salamis. If you are on a budget, consider snacking on stuzzichini with a few drinks during happy hour which is often between 7 and 9pm. The fare can include salami, cheeses, cured meat, mini pizzas, bread, vegetables, pastries or pate. In Italy, Parmesan refers only to cheese originating from the area surrounding Parma. Favorites desserts include tiramisu or Italian gelato.

Italians enjoy relaxing to aperitifs before they settle down to a meal and their favorites are Campari, Aperol or Negroni, the famous Italian cocktail. Wine is enjoyed with dinner. Italy is particularly famous for its red wines. The best known wine regions are Piedmont, which produces robust and dry reds, Tuscany and Alto Adige, where Alpine soil adds a distinctive acidity. After the meal, they settle down to a glass of limoncello, the country's most popular liqueur, or grappa, which is distilled from grape seeds and stems, as digestive. Other options in this class include a nut liqueur, nocino, strawberry based Fragolino Veneto or herbal digestives like gineprino, laurino or mirto. Italians are also fond of coffee. Espresso is drunk through throughout the day, but cappuccino is considered a morning drink. The most popular beers in Italy are Peroni and Moretti.

Websites

http://vistoperitalia.esteri.it/home/en

This is the website of the Consulate General of Italy. Here you can look up whether you will need a visa and also process your application online.

http://www.italia.it/en/home.html

The official website of Italian tourism

http://www.italia.it/en/useful-info/mobile-apps.html

Select the region of your choice to download a useful mobile app to your phone.

http://www.italylogue.com/tourism

http://italiantourism.com/index.html

http://www.reidsitaly.com/

http://wikitravel.org/en/Italy

https://www.summerinitaly.com/

http://www.accessibleitalianholiday.com/

Planning Italian vacations around the needs of disabled tourists.

Printed in Great Britain
by Amazon